Illustrations by
Loren Jones

The BOOK of ANSWERS

According to

TAYLOR

Quadrille

INTRODUCTION

Taylor Swift is an icon to millions of people for her sparkling songwriting and the joy she brings onstage. Her Eras Tour smashed records and became a cultural phenomenon. The sheer joy she inspires is probably why her fans are so devoted, following her every move and bringing up the topic of her music at every party (sorry non-Swifties). Despite being a powerhouse popstar and global celebrity, she somehow never feels out of reach. Her songs are the soundtrack to our dance parties, road trips and getting ready sessions. Her Track Fives are so good they almost make it worth going through a breakup. Whether you're feeling the tender beginnings of falling in love or going through the misery of a broken heart, Taylor's songs become like best friends who stick with you through the highs and lows of life.

So what can we learn from Taylor? She has proved herself to be resilient and strong in the face of bullying and criticism. Like many of us, she was unsure of herself when she was starting out. She entered the music industry at a very young age and although she was very determined to succeed, she also felt pressured to meet people's expectations of a demure young lady. She didn't always know that she had the right to stand up for herself or express her opinion in public. Eventually, she realised that she needed to defend herself and fight for what was right, or powerful people in the industry would take advantage of her. Over time she has faced down big companies and obnoxious people with grace and patience, and survived a series of backlashes. She has channeled her rage and frustration into her music. All the while, she has never lost sight of what makes her unique: her ability to put love, heartbreak, sadness and triumph into songs. Time has proved that she is the best at what she does.

Although Taylor is a generation-defining star, she's a real person with feelings who has been through situations many of us can relate to. Luckily for us, she has described her emotions in aching detail. We all know what it is like to feel rejected by friends or love interests, worry that we'll never find love, or wonder if we can bounce back from disaster or is everything *ruined forever*? Taylor proves that you can not only survive difficult situations but emerge from them better than ever. We all have our *reputation* eras and we make it through to see the daylight.

Affirmations and encouraging advice can really help with navigating life. This book imagines what advice Taylor would give you when you're feeling lost or facing a dilemma. Put yourself in her shoes and imagine yourself as a powerful woman in glittery boots, who is very in touch with her creativity and emotions. Put on your favourite Taylor song and ask "what would Taylor do?" Then flip to a random page for a little bit of her wisdom.

TRUST IN TAYLOR TO EMPOWER YOU ON LIFE'S JOURNEY

HOW TO USE THIS BOOK

The Book of Answers invites us to uncover Taylor Swifts' wisdom and model it in our own lives. When there are hard decisions to be made or you need some positive words, tap into the power of this magical icon to find the answers you have been searching for.

※ Press play on your favourite Taylor Swift song.

※ Breathe deeply for three counts as Taylor begins to sing, holding the closed book next to your heart.

※ Allow Taylor's voice to enter your mind and focus on your question.

※ See the question in your mind's eye or say or sing it aloud.

※ Run a finger along all the page edges and when you feel called, stop and open the book in that place. This is Taylor's answer to you.

SHAKE IT OFF BABE.

IT'S NOT
TOO MUCH:
WEAR THE
RED LIPSTICK.

Seize the

moment.

DANCE AROUND YOUR BEDROOM.

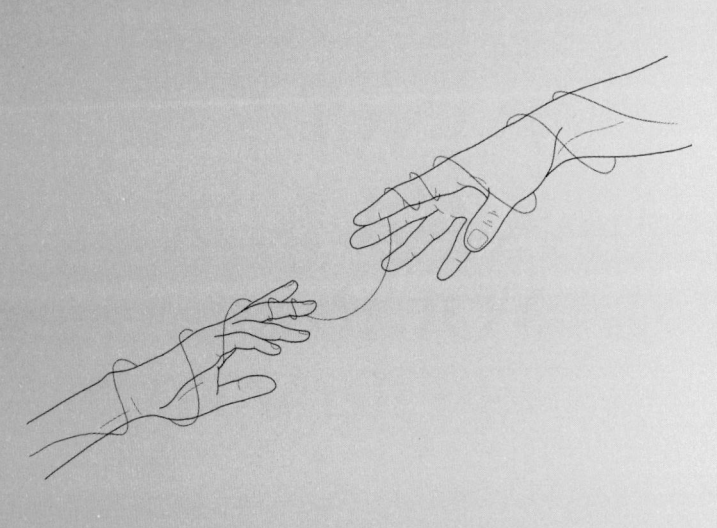

NOTHING IS
AS BAD ONCE
YOU'VE TALKED
ABOUT IT.

YOU'RE ALLOWED TO LET IT GO.

YOU DID YOUR BEST IN THE MOMENT.

YOU ARE
A TRULY
KIND AND
CONSIDERATE
FRIEND.

Love is in

your stars.

YOU DESERVE NICE THINGS.

YOU DESERVE
THE TRUEST
OF LOVES.

ALL YOUR
WILDEST
DREAMS WILL
COME TRUE.

DON'T GET MAD, GET EVEN.

YOU ARE STRONG ENOUGH TO FACE THIS.

THINGS WILL GET BETTER.

TOMORROW IS
A BLANK SLATE.

Write your

own story.

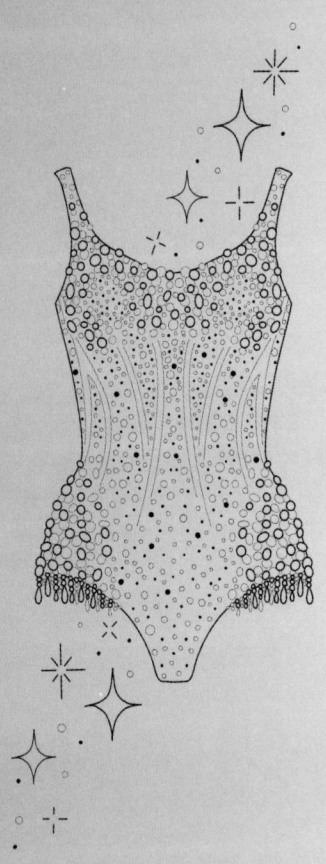

THERE IS ONLY ONE OF YOU.

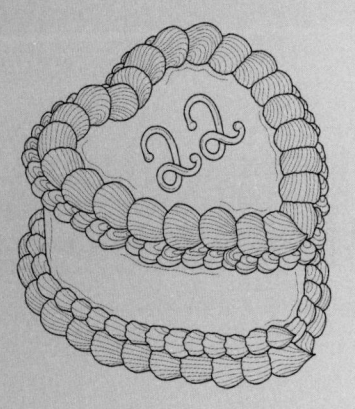

YOU ARE SO RESILIENT.

YOUR WORDS DESERVE TO BE HEARD.

YOU ARE A SPARKLING STAR.

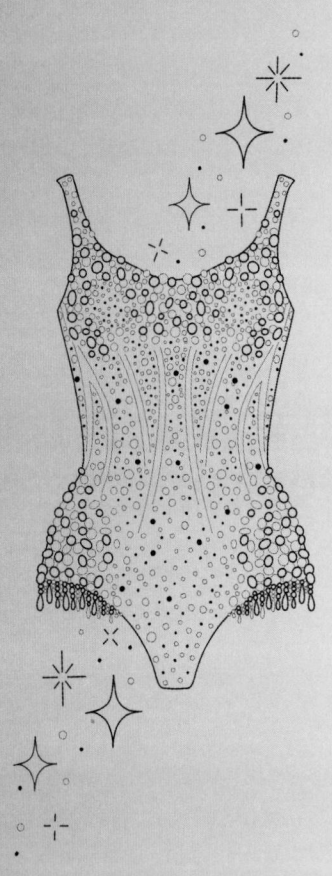

YOU SHINE LIKE FIREWORKS.

YOU HAVE SUCH
A GOOD HEART.

YOU ARE
FEARLESS.

Stay classy,

no matter

what.

LEARN FROM YOUR SETBACKS AND COME BACK STRONGER.

You survived your

reputation era.

BELIEVE IN
YOURSELF,
LIKE I BELIEVE
IN YOU.

FALL IN LOVE WITH YOUR LIFE.

TODAY IS GOING TO BE THE BEST DAY.

YOU CAN DO IT,
EVEN WITH A
BROKEN HEART.

Cherish this moment.

ENJOY THE SPOTLIGHT.

You are

a queen

(or a king).

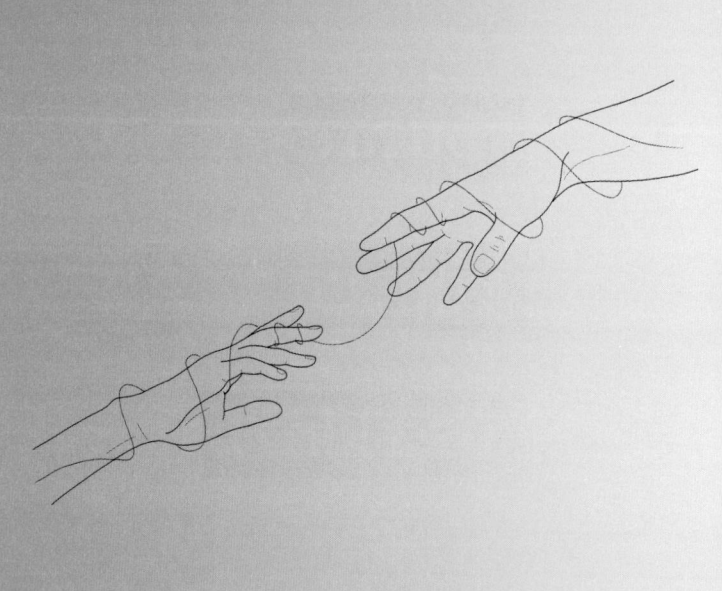

AFTER THE
DARKEST NIGHT,
THERE WILL
BE DAYLIGHT.

YOU DESERVE EVERY HAPPINESS.

YOU ARE STILL BEJEWELED.

You get
a little bit
better every
single day.

LEAVE THE PAST IN THE PAST.

YOU'RE GOING TO FEEL BETTER, SOON.

GET
UP AND
DANCE.

SAY WHAT YOU'VE BEEN THINKING.

YOUR FEELINGS ARE NEVER TOO MUCH.

Wear your prettiest dress today, just because.

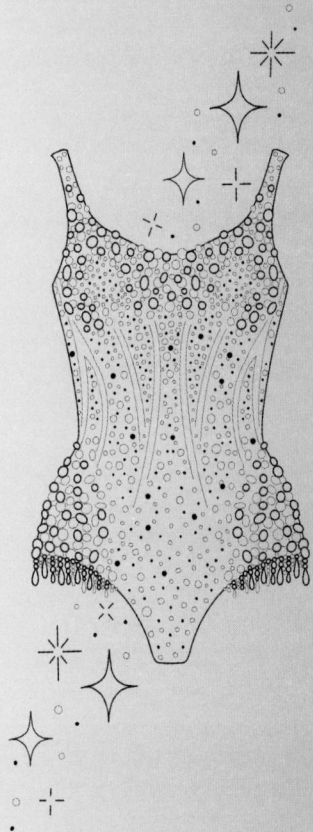

YOU ARE
ENCHANTING.

YOU'RE NOT ON YOUR OWN.

HAPPINESS IS RIGHT AROUND THE CORNER.

TRUST IN THE UNIVERSE.

YOUR MISTAKES
ARE JUST A
SMALL PART
OF YOUR STORY.

Your chosen

family

loves you.

THIS IS YOUR BEST ERA YET.

LEAVE BEHIND
THINGS THAT
NO LONGER
WORK FOR YOU.

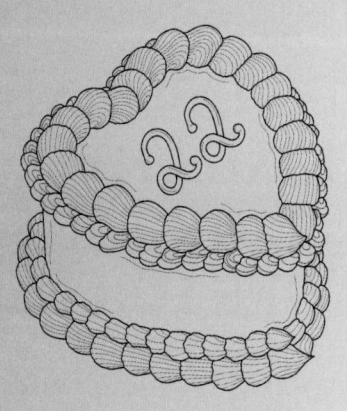

BE THE LOVE OF YOUR OWN LIFE.

YOU'RE A GOOD LISTENER.

You're

a lucky

person.

YOU'RE THE MAN.

YOU HAVE THE BEST IDEAS.

YOU ARE COMPLEX *AND* COOL.

AFTER THE RAIN, THERE WILL BE A RAINBOW.

Sing at the top of your lungs.

YOU
ARE THE
SMARTEST
PERSON
I KNOW.

GLITTER LIKE A MIRRORBALL.

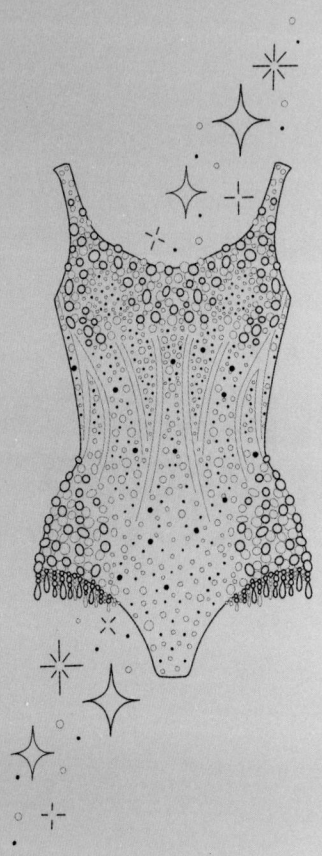

YOU THROW THE BEST PARTIES.

Get back up

and try again.

YOU CAN CHANGE YOUR FUTURE. START TODAY!

TELL THEM HOW YOU FEEL.

Your

vulnerability

is a

superpower.

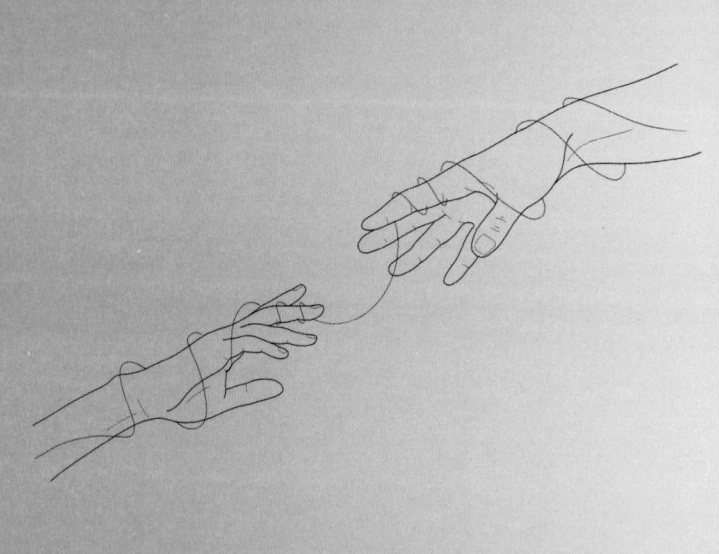

I'VE GOT YOUR BACK.

YOU
ARE
SAFE.

IGNORE THE HATERS.

TRUST PEOPLE,
BUT IF SOMEONE
COMES AT YOU,
BE READY.

STAND UP FOR YOURSELF.

STAND UP FOR OTHER PEOPLE.

Believe

in your

ideas.

YOU'RE ALREADY SO STRONG.

SPEAK
OUT.

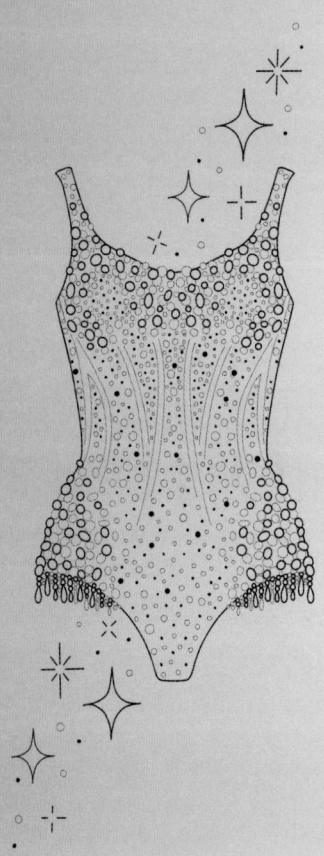

You never go

out of style.

I LOVE
YOUR
LOOK.

YOU'RE
A FUTURE
SUPERSTAR.

Let the trash take itself out.

TRY YOUR BEST.

CHOOSE
TO STAY.

You are

different,

in a good way.

You're unique!

WHAT IS MEANT FOR YOU WILL COME BACK TO YOU.

You deserve

a big love.

FEEL IT ALL.

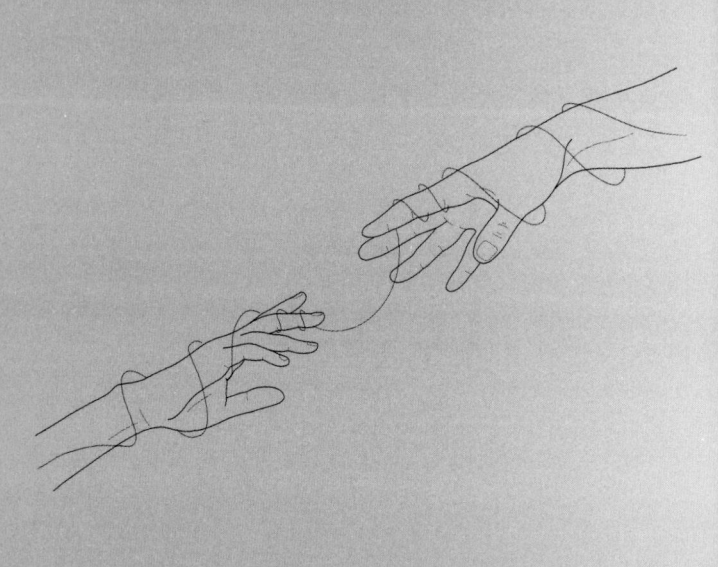

LOVE WITH YOUR WHOLE HEART.

You can

always begin

again.

TOMORROW IS A NEW DAY.

YOU ARE
YOUR OWN
PRINCE
CHARMING.

Don't play
it safe. Follow
your dreams.

SHOOT YOUR SHOT. YOU NEVER KNOW!

YOU BELONG HERE.

YOU ARE READY FOR LOVE.

Someone

loves you,

I promise.

WRITE IT ALL DOWN.

IF IT'S NOT WORKING, MOVE ON.

MASTERMIND
YOUR OWN LIFE.

Happiness is your greatest success.

SPIN IN YOUR HIGHEST HEELS.

You are so

talented.

I can see you

going far.

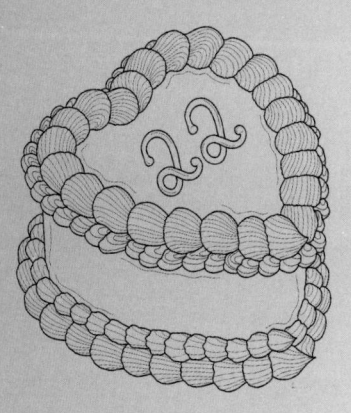

CHOOSE
TO SEE THE
BRIGHT SIDE.

MOVE ON TO YOUR NEXT ERA.

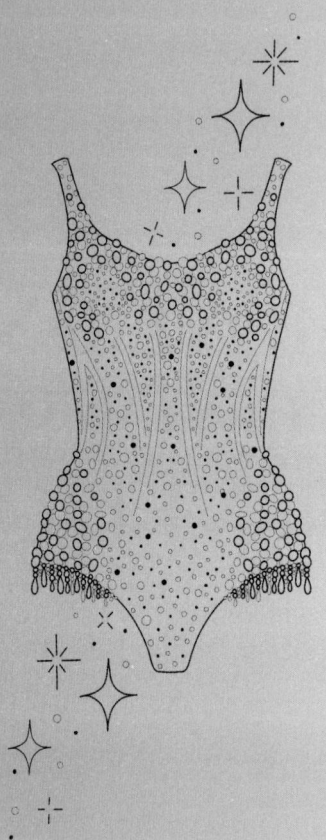

Mentally wear

a glittery

bodysuit and

heels at all times.

LEARN TO LIVE ALONGSIDE CRINGE.

DEFINE YOURSELF BY WHAT YOU LOVE.

Your likes

and loves

are valid.

DON'T COMPARE
YOURSELF
TO OTHERS –
EVERYONE HAS
THEIR OWN
UNIQUE CROWN.

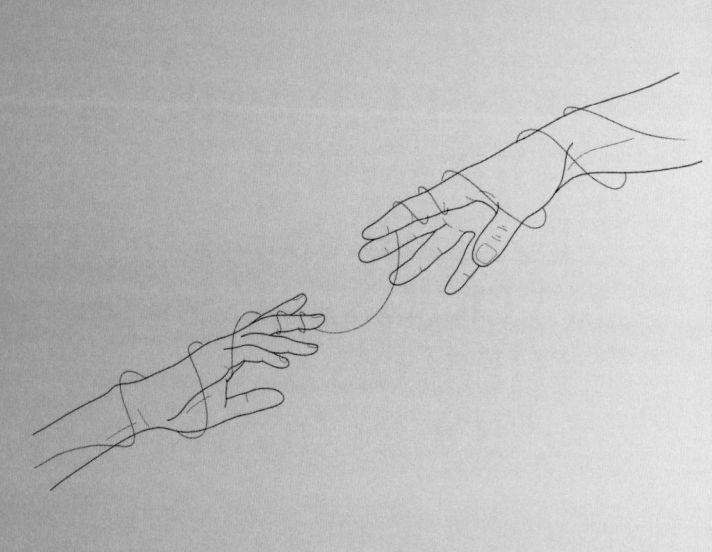

BLOCK OUT THE NOISE.

TAKE A REAL BREAK.

Trust your instincts.

YOUR TIME BELONGS TO YOU.

YOU HAVE THE
LAST WORD ON
YOUR OWN LIFE.

PEOPLE ARE
GOING TO JUDGE
YOU ANYWAY,
SO YOU MIGHT
AS WELL DO
WHAT YOU WANT.

YOU WILL
FIND PEACE.

Just

block

them.

YOU HAVE TO TAKE RISKS TO GROW.

ACCEPT YOUR
BODY AS IT IS.
YOU NEED THAT
HEADSPACE FOR
GREATER THINGS.

DON'T LET ANYONE ANYONE DRAIN YOU OF ENERGY.

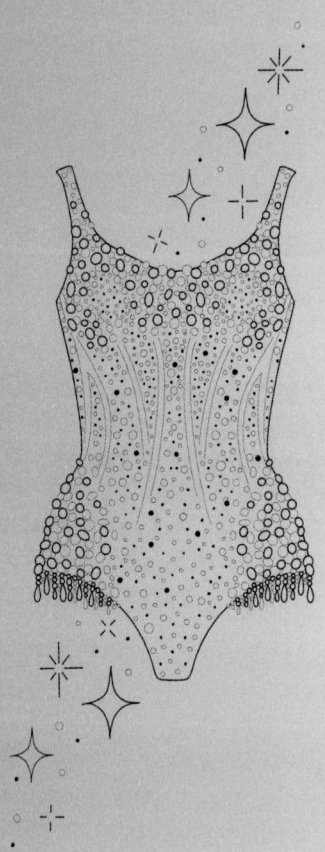

Protect

your

spark.

CELEBRATE
GETTING OLDER.
IT IS NORMAL
AND FINE AND
KIND OF GREAT.

Make peace

with your

worst fears.

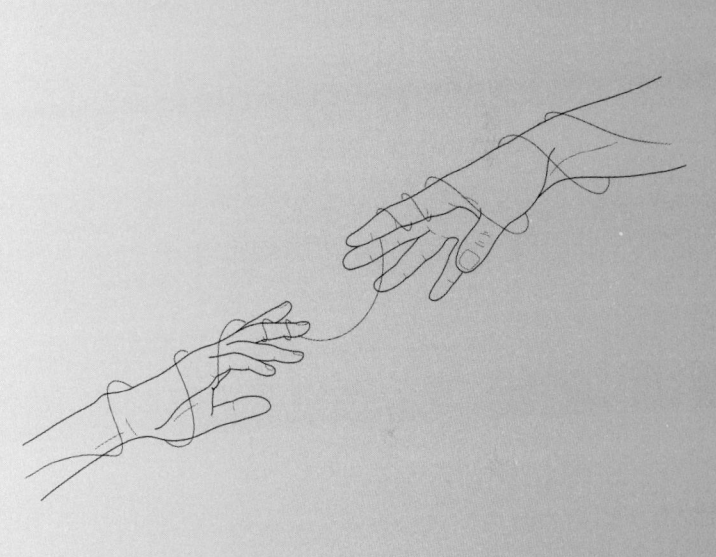

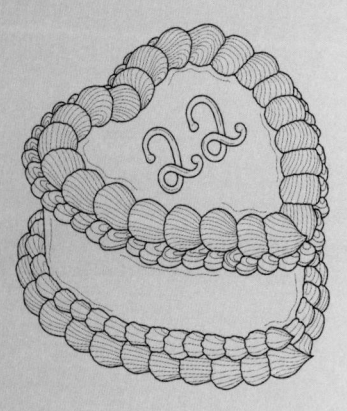

YOUR MIDDLE-
OF-THE-NIGHT
THOUGHTS WILL
BE GONE BY
THE MORNING.

YOU CAN ONLY CONTROL YOUR OWN ACTIONS.

ONE PERSON'S REJECTION DOESN'T DEFINE YOU.

It's okay:

you can

say sorry.

Don't bottle it up.

Tell someone.

YOUR INSECURITIES
AREN'T YOUR
WHOLE STORY.

YOU'RE
NOT BAD;
YOU'RE NOT
PERFECT;
YOU'RE JUST
HUMAN.

YOUR HAIR WILL
GROW BACK AFTER
A BAD HAIRCUT.

PUT DOWN
THAT ARMFUL
OF TINY WORRIES
YOU'RE CARRYING.
YOU'VE GOT A
BIG LIFE TO LIVE.

Seize the moment.

CHOOSE TO BE HAPPY.

STOP BEING
SO HARD ON
YOURSELF RIGHT
THIS MINUTE
YOUNG LADY.

You're already

good enough.

YOU DESERVE
TO LET LOVE IN.

LOVE IS ABOUT
TO SHOW UP
AT YOUR DOOR,
POSSIBLY COMING
IN FROM THE RAIN.

Keep

wishing

on a star.

FORGIVE
YOURSELF.

Don't forget

to thank the

support team.

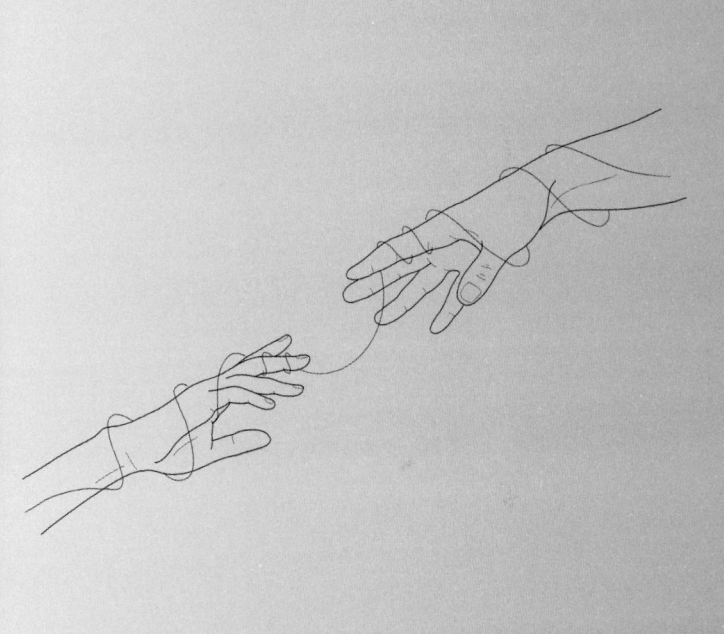

YOU ARE READY FOR IT.

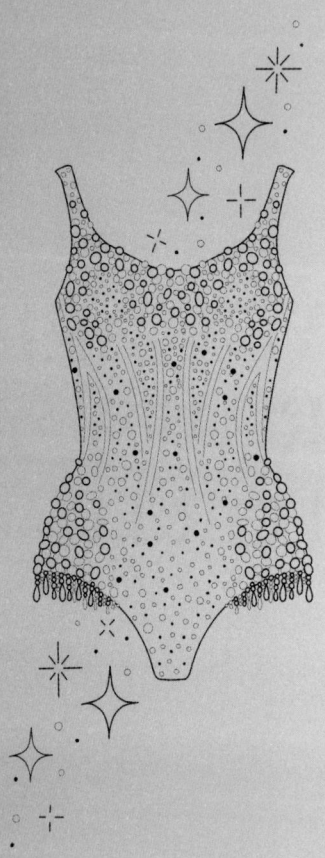

YOU ARE HAVING THE TIME OF YOUR LIFE.

YOU WILL
ACHIEVE
YOUR GOALS.

You are

tougher than

you look.

EVEN ON YOUR
HARDEST DAYS,
YOU DO WHAT
NEEDS TO BE DONE.

You are

a winner.

YOU ARE SO PRODUCTIVE.

You are

powerful and

ambitious.

TRUST YOURSELF TO DO WHAT'S BEST FOR YOU.

THERE ARE NO LIMITS ON WHAT YOU CAN ACHIEVE.

Ask for help when you need it.

RESPECT YOUR OWN JUDGMENT.

KNOW WHAT IS MEANT FOR YOU.

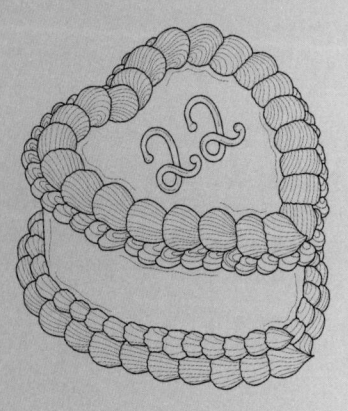

ACCEPT THE TRUTH WHEN YOU HEAR IT.

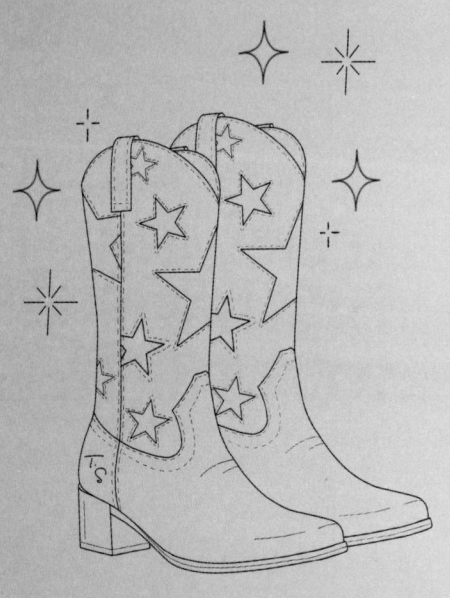

YOUR SELF-WORTH
IS NOT DECIDED
BY PRAISE FROM
OTHERS, NOT EVEN
THE GRAMMY AWARDS.

Take a real

rest day.

YOU DON'T CHASE
LOVE, YOU FIND
IT WHEN THE
TIME IS RIGHT.

JUST
SAY
YES.

Have faith
in people.

YOU KNOW WHAT TO DO NEXT.

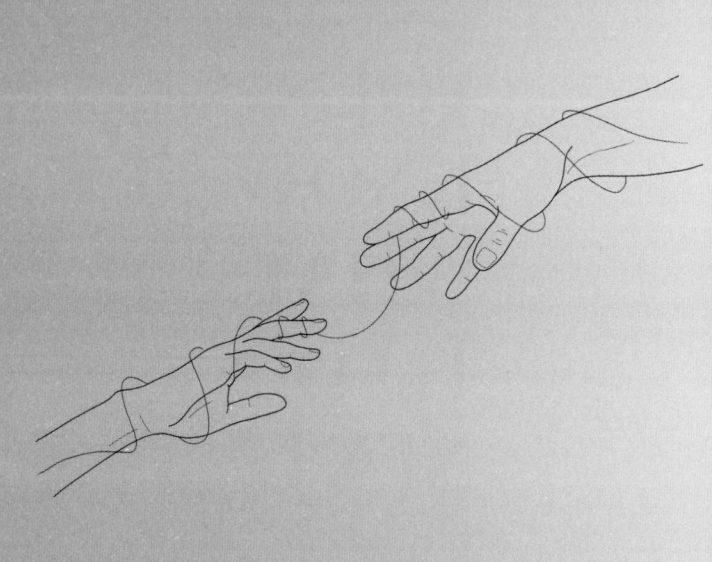

THERE IS AN INVISIBLE STRING LEADING YOU TO HAPPINESS.

Take it

one day

at at time.

RELAX –
IT'S GOING
TO BE OKAY.

You can come
back from
disaster, better
than ever.

NO ONE CAN HOLD YOU BACK.

YOU PRIORITISE
THE PEOPLE YOU
LOVE AND WHO
LOVE YOU BACK.

NO ONE CAN STEAL YOUR PEACEFULNESS.

DON'T LET ANYONE PUT YOU DOWN.

Own

the

room.

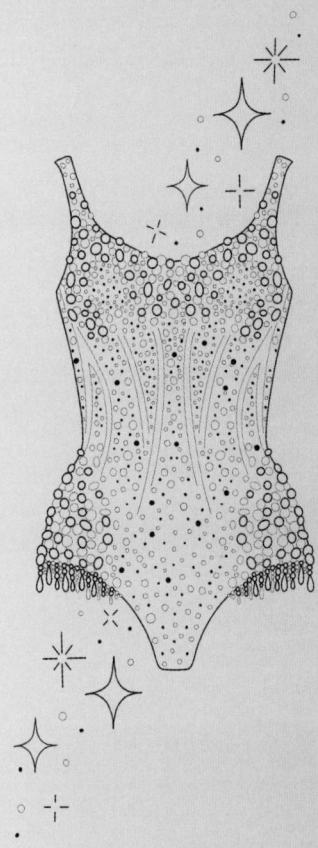

YOUR PAST
DOESN'T
DEFINE YOU
IF YOU DON'T
LET IT.

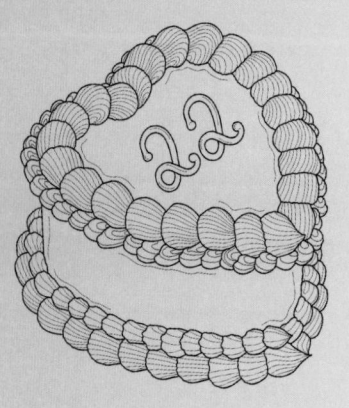

YOU DON'T NEED TO PERSUADE EVERYONE YOU'RE RIGHT.

Not everyone

will like you

and that's okay.

YOU ARE NEEDED
IN THE WORLD
(THE TAYLOR
SWIFT FANDOM).

BEING BAD AT
SOMETHING
DOESN'T MAKE
YOU BAD.

Build the

life *you* want.

YOU WILL GET TICKETS TO THE NEXT TOUR.

TAKE UP
SPACE.

STATE YOUR
OPINION EVEN
IF PEOPLE
DON'T LIKE IT.

STAND UP TO BULLIES.

Don't pretend
to be someone
you're not.

YOU WILL FIND YOUR PEOPLE.

**YOUR FRIENDS
LIKE YOU THE
WAY YOU ARE.**

When things change around you, embrace it as a new era.

PLAN FUN
THINGS
BUT LEAVE
SPACE FOR
SURPRISES.

Wear whatever you want.

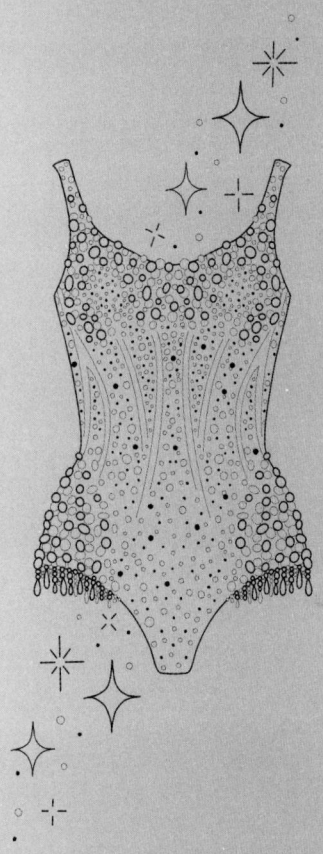

FEEL YOUR FEELINGS AND NEVER TRY TO DENY THEM.

BEING SENSITIVE IS A GIFT.

FORGIVE
YOURSELF
FOR THAT ONE
THING YOU
DID. IT'S TIME
TO MOVE ONE.

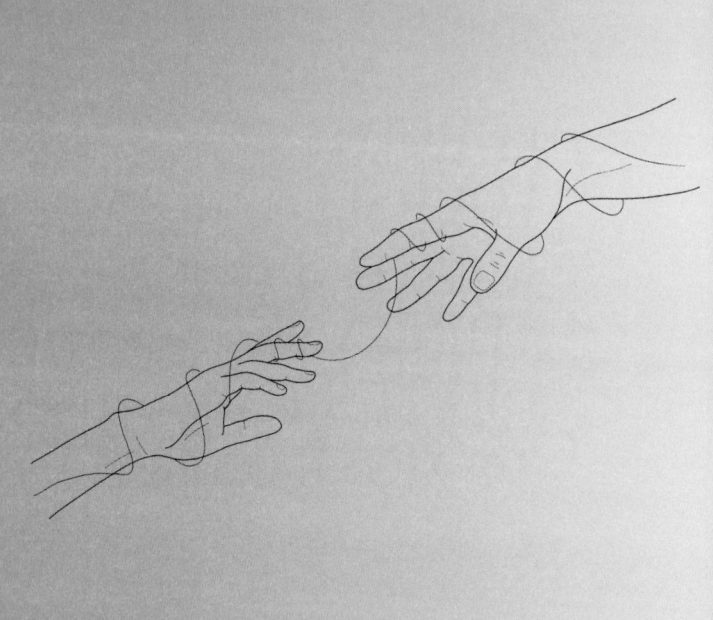

Love can

come in all

sorts of forms.

TAKE TIME
TO RECHARGE
AFTER A BIG
MOMENT.

GO TO THE
PARTIES YOU'RE
EXCITED ABOUT
AND SKIP THE
ONES YOU'RE NOT.

It's your life and

only you can decide

what to do with it.

GET SWEPT AWAY EVERY NOW AND THEN.

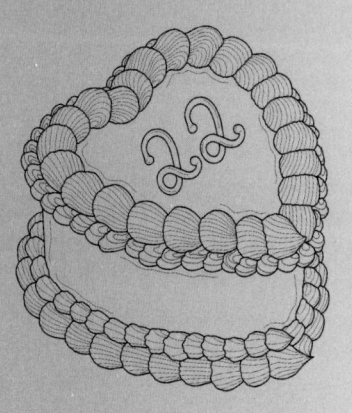

BOTH HAPPINESS
AND UNHAPPINESS
ARE BETTER
WHEN SHARED.

TAKE A DEEP BREATH.

It's okay to

do (sweet)

nothing

sometimes.

YOU MAKE
BEING
AMAZING
LOOK EASY.

399

YOUR ANXIETY DOESN'T OWN YOU.

EVEN ON YOUR WORST DAY, YOU ARE LOVEABLE.

You are the main

character of

your own story.

404

YOU CAN BE SOFT
AND INCREDIBLY
TOUGH AT THE
SAME TIME.

DON'T GIVE UP.
THOSE OBSTACLES
WILL LOOK SO
SMALL IN THE
REARVIEW
MIRROR ONE DAY.

YOU ARE
SO LOYAL
TO YOUR
FRIENDS.

Other people

see the

beauty in you.

EVERYONE
PICKS THE
WRONG
FIRST SINGLE
SOMETIMES.

LOVE IS NOT IN SHORT SUPPLY.

You can be kind

and clever at

the same time.

YOU CAN BE BOTH POWERFUL AND POLITE.

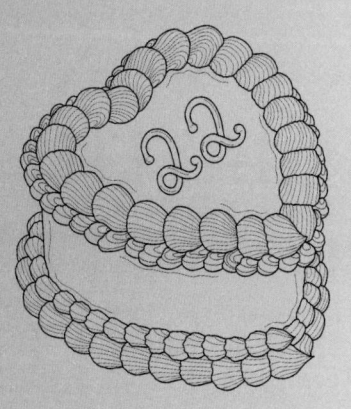

Day by day,

month by month,

heartbreak gets

a little easier.

THAT TRICKY
SITUATION
CAN WAIT UNTIL
TOMORROW.

YOU ARE NOT
IN CONTROL
OF EVERYTHING.

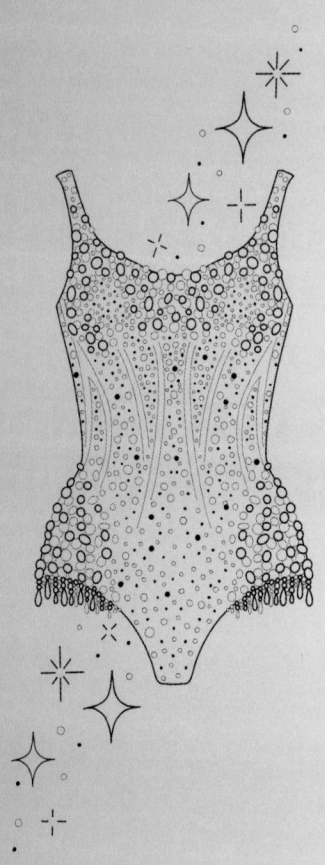

YOU ARE
MAGICAL.

You can

slay dragons

if you put your

mind to it.

YOUR STORY
IS A FAIRYTALE.

YOU ARE YOUR OWN HERO.

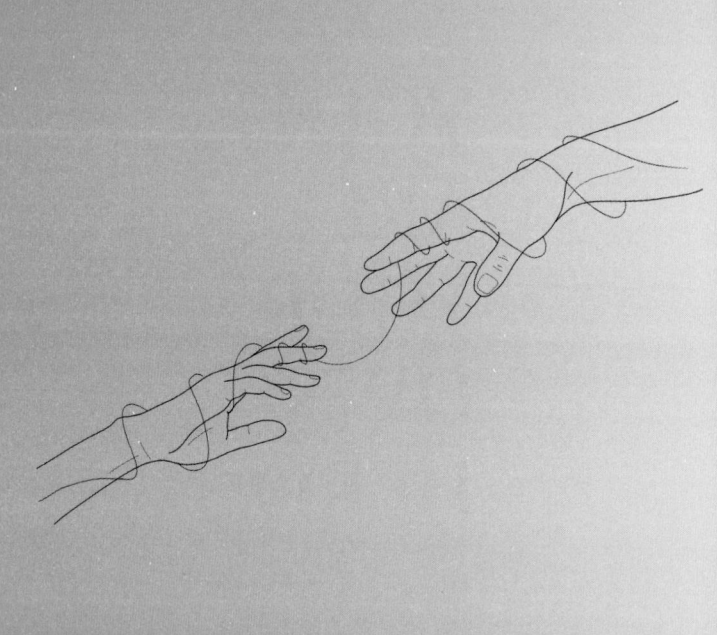

TAKE GOOD CARE
OF YOURSELF.
YOU NEED ENERGY
FOR ALL THOSE
AMAZING THINGS
YOU'RE GOING
TO DO.

SMILE FROM EAR
TO EAR, DANCE LIKE
A CHILD, SING LIKE
NO ONE CAN HEAR
YOU AND LOVE
LIKE IT'S YOUR LAST
DAY ON EARTH.

Other people's judgement is none of your business.

NURTURE YOUR CREATIVITY.

IF YOU CAN'T SAY IT, WRITE IT DOWN.

Other people's

bad behaviour

is not your fault.

YOU DESERVE TO
BE PROTECTED.

449

Allow yourself

moments

of pure joy.

LOVE CAN BE
WILD, PEACEFUL,
PASSIONATE OR
COMFORTABLE,
AND YOU
DESERVE IT ALL.

LIFE IS A JOURNEY.
SOMETIMES YOU
HAVE TO GO
BACKWARDS TO
END UP MAKING
PROGRESS.

IF YOU STAY IN YOUR COMFORT ZONE, YOU'LL NEVER EXPERIENCE ALL LIFE HAS TO OFFER.

Go after what

you want with

all your might.

DON'T
LET YOUR
REGRETS
RULE
YOUR LIFE.

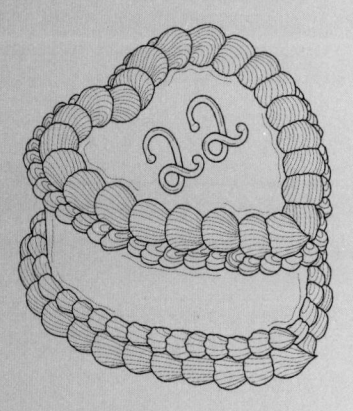

Stand up

for what you

believe in.

EVERYONE
DESERVES
A SECOND
CHANCE
BUT NOT A
THIRD ONE.

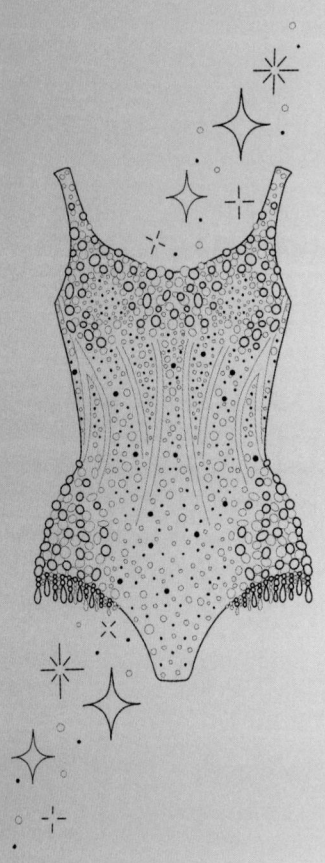

NO ONE'S TASTE
IN MUSIC IS
BETTER THAN
ANYONE ELSE'S.
JUST ENJOY
YOURSELF.

True friends

like you for you.

DON'T WORRY ABOUT YOUR SO-CALLED REPUTATION.

YOU'RE NOT
WRONG,
YOU'RE JUST
AHEAD OF
THE CURVE.

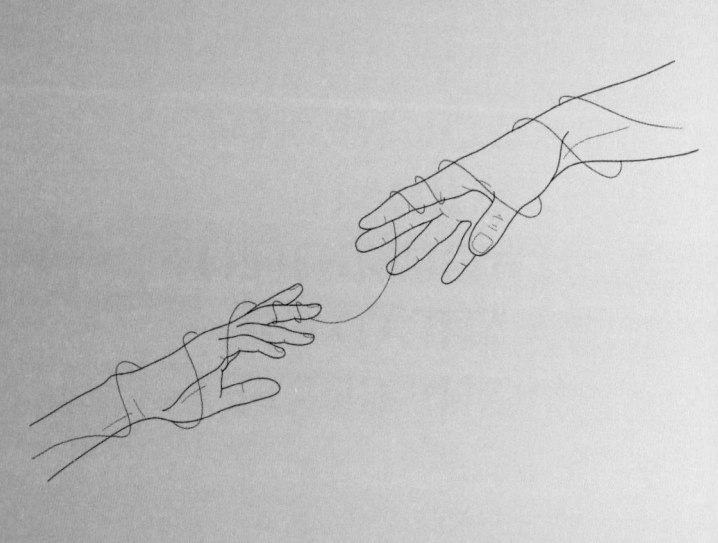

YOU MAY NEVER
TRULY GET OVER
YOUR FIRST LOVE,
BUT YOU WILL
GROW BEYOND IT.

You are not

a footnote

in someone

else's life.

IT'S OKAY IF
YOU'RE NOT
OVER IT YET.

YOU'RE NOT LOST, YOU JUST HAVEN'T FOUND YOUR CALLING YET.

Leave all the

negativity behind.

YOU CAN MOVE PAST YOUR PAST LIVES.

485

Your past

mistakes will

be forgiven.

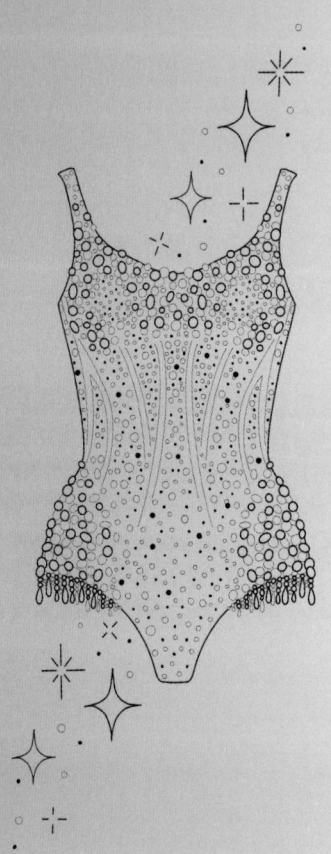

BE KIND,
BE HONEST,
BE STRONG,
AND SURROUND
YOURSELF
WITH GOOD
PEOPLE.

THE RIGHT PERSON WILL PUT YOU IN THE PENTHOUSE.

Time will help

you let go of

your grudges.

BE MINDFUL
OF HOW YOUR
WORDS CAN
WOUND PEOPLE.

YOU DON'T
HAVE TO SHARE
EVERYTHING
WITH FRIENDS,
FAMILY OR
THE WORLD.

BE LIKE A SNAKE –
ONLY BITE
IF SOMEONE
STEPS ON YOU.

YOU DON'T HAVE
TO FORGIVE AND
YOU DON'T HAVE
TO FORGET TO
MOVE ON.

Decide what is
yours to hold and
let the rest go.

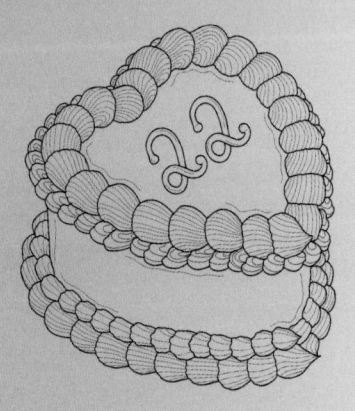

MAKE FRIENDSHIP BRACELETS.

505

You deserve

a good time.

TALK TO YOURSELF LIKE YOU'D TALK TO YOUR BEST FRIEND.

YOU ARE GOLDEN,
LIKE DAYLIGHT.

Quadrille, Penguin Random House UK, One Embassy
Gardens, 8 Viaduct Gardens, London SW11 7BW

Quadrille Publishing Limited is part of the Penguin
Random House group of companies whose addresses
can be found at: global.penguinrandomhouse.com

ISBN 9781837833955
10 9 8 7 6 5 4 3 2 1

Publishing Director: Kate Pollard
Senior Commissioning Editor: Kate Burkett
Designer: Claire Warner Studio
Production Controller: Martina Georgieva
Written by: Satu Fox

Colour reproduction by p2d

Printed in China by RR Donnelley Asia Printing
Solution Limited

The authorised representative in the EEA is
Penguin Random House Ireland, Morrison Chambers,
32 Nassau Street, Dublin D02 YH68.

Published by Quadrille in 2025

www.penguin.co.uk

A CIP catalogue record for this book
is available from the British Library

Page 215   NYU commencement speech
Page 499   https://www.elle.com/culture/celebrities/a26628467/taylor-swift-30th-birthday-lessons/
Page 501   https://www.cbsnews.com/news/taylor-swift-on-lover-and-haters/
Page 502   NYU commencement speech